Spirit be joyful!

14 songs for Advent and Christmas

for high voice and piano or organ

Compiled and translated by Jane Marsh

MUSIC DEPARTMENT

OXFORD
UNIVERSITY PRESS

UNIVERSITY PRESS

198 Madison Avenue, New York, NY 10016, USA
Great Clarendon Street, Oxford OX2 6DP, England

Oxford University Press is a department of the University of Oxford.
It furthers the University's aim of excellence in research, scholarship,
and education by publishing worldwide

Oxford New York
Auckland Bangkok Buenos Aires Cape Town Chennai
Dar es Salaam Delhi Hong Kong Istanbul Karachi Kolkata
Kuala Lumpur Madrid Melbourne Mexico City Mumbai Nairobi
São Paulo Shanghai Taipei Tokyo Toronto

Oxford is a registered trademark of Oxford University Press

© Oxford University Press, Inc. 2008

Database right Oxford University Press (maker)

First published 2008

All rights reserved. No part of this publication may be reproduced,
stored in a retrieval system, or transmitted, in any form or by any means,
without the prior permission in writing of Oxford University Press,
or as expressly permitted by law. Enquiries concerning reproduction
outside the scope of the above should be sent to the Music
Department, Oxford University Press, at the address above

Permission to perform the works in this anthology in public
(except in the course of divine worship) should normally be obtained
from the American Society of Composers, Authors and Publishers (ASCAP),
One Lincoln Plaza, New York, NY 10023, or its affiliated Societies in each
country throughout the world, unless the owner or the occupier of the
premises being used holds a license from the Society

Permission to make a sound recording must be obtained in advance from
The Harry Fox Agency, 711 Third Avenue, New York, NY, 10017,
or its affiliated Societies in each country throughout the world.

1 3 5 7 9 10 8 6 4 2

ISBN 978-0-19-537350-9

Music origination by Enigma Music Production Services, Amersham, Bucks, UK
Printed in the United States of America on acid-free paper

Every effort has been made to trace copyright owners and apologies are
extended to any whose rights have inadvertently not been acknowledged.
Any omissions or inaccuracies of copyright detail will be corrected
in subsequent printings if brought to the publisher's attention.

Contents

CD Acknowledgements	iii
Preface	iv
1. **J. S. Bach** – Mein gläubiges Herze frohlocke (My reverent spirit, be joyful)	1
2. **Ludwig van Beethoven** – Hymne an die Nacht (Hymn to the Night)	5
3. **Bob Chilcott** – The Time of Snow	6
4. **Peter Cornelius** – Die Hirten (The Shepherds)	10
5. **Gabriel Fauré** – Noël (Christmas)	12
6. **Engelbert Humperdinck** – Weihnachten (Christmas)	16
7. **J. C. G. Loewe** – Der Hirten Lied am Krippelein (The Shepherds' Song at the Little Crib)	20
8. **Modest Mussorgsky** – Molitva (Prayer)	23
9. **Max Reger** – Maria am Rosenstrauch (Mary at the Rose Shrub)	26
10. **Ottorino Respighi** – Venitelo a vedere 'l mi' piccino (O come and look at him, my little baby)	28
11. **Franz Schubert** – Die Allmacht (The Almighty)	31
12. **Robert Schumann** – Weihnachtlied (Christmas Song)	37
13. **Giuseppe Verdi** – Ave Maria (Hail Mary)	38
14. **Hugo Wolf** – Schlafendes Jesuskind (Sleeping Jesus Child)	42

CD Acknowledgements

The CD contains a backing track for each piece and selected performance tracks. We are grateful to the following musicians for performing on the CD: Norman Carey, piano; Nadine Earl Carey, soprano (track 15); Jane Marsh, soprano (tracks 16–21). Engineer: John P. Hopkins. Recorded at Lofish Productions Inc., New York, June 30–July 2, 2008.

 This symbol, which appears at the top of the first page of music for each piece, indicates the relevant CD track numbers for each piece. The top number indicates the backing (accompaniment) track and the bottom number the relevant performance track, if available.

Preface

This anthology attempts to provide a new song collection that is inspirational, fun, and productive for everyone involved in the celebration of Advent and Christmas, whether in a church service or a recital hall. This collection abounds in thematic, stylistic, linguistic, and musical diversity providing both students and professionals with new repertoire for performance. The composers featured in this collection are well known for their standard repertoire, but these selections, written in celebration of this joyous season, are lesser known and can offer new and innovative material. It is my hope that singers might rediscover these little gems and incorporate them into their repertoire, to the delight of the listener.

This collection brings together selections from Germany, Russia, Italy, France, and the United Kingdom. Though I strongly encourage every singer to experience singing repertoire in the original languages, I have written new, poetic singing translations for those who prefer to sing these songs in English. In addition, the translations can help the performer understand the original text. Mussorgsky's song *Molitva*, with Russian text by Lermontov, includes my added Russian transliteration and enunciation guide for immediacy in reading and singing.

Recitals on the theme of Advent and Christmas are popular throughout the world, and I would like to suggest two possible formats in which the material in this collection might be programmed.

The first format, with no intermission, features all of the selections from this anthology arranged into three groups with the entire program lasting approximately 45 minutes. Group 1: Bach, Beethoven, Cornelius, and Fauré. Group 2: Loewe, Wolf, Reger, Schumann, and Schubert. Group 3: Mussorgsky, Chilcott, Respighi, Verdi, and Humperdinck.

The second format presents a recital that would last 70–80 minutes, would include an intermission, and would require incorporating music outside of this collection. The first half would focus on a particular poet or composer. For example, one could feature Schubert and Wolf's settings of Goethe's poetry. Group 1: Five settings by Schubert. Group 2: Five settings by Wolf, ending with Wolf's *Epiphanias* (Epiphany) which would serve as the pivotal song pointing to the Advent and Christmas second half of the program. A second option for the first half would be to feature Mahler's *Des Knaben Wunderhorn* (The Youth's Magic Horn). Group 1: Three or four selections from *Lieder der Jugendzeit* (Songs of the time of youth). Group 2: Three or four selections from *Des Knaben Wunderhorn* originally scored for orchestra but performed with piano. Group 3: The piano version of the 4th Movement, *Wir geniessen die himmlischen Freuden* (We enjoy the joys of heaven), from Mahler's 4th Symphony. This last selection would also serve as the pivotal song pointing to the Advent and Christmas second half of the program. The second half of the program would consist of selections from this anthology in these suggested groupings; Group 1: Verdi, Bach, Cornelius, and Fauré. Group 2: Wolf, Loewe, Reger, and Schubert. Group 3: Chilcott, Respighi, and Humperdinck.

Much joy and success with your Advent and Christmas programming.

JANE MARSH
July 2008

1. Mein gläubiges Herze frohlocke
My reverent spirit, be joyful

Cantata # 68
trans. Jane Marsh

J. S. BACH
(1685–1750)

This collection and this piece © 2008 Oxford University Press, Inc. Photocopying this copyright material is ILLEGAL.

2. Hymne an die Nacht
Hymn to the Night

Hosianna # 161
Liturgical text
trans. Jane Marsh

LUDWIG VAN BEETHOVEN
(1770–1827)

This hymn and the second movement of Beethoven's piano sonata "Appassionata" (Op. 57) share the same thematic material.

Copyright © 2008, Oxford University Press, Inc. Photocopying this copyright material is ILLEGAL.

3. The Time of Snow

Words and music
BOB CHILCOTT
(b. 1955)

They jour-ney on - ward to find their rest,

Ma-ry and Jo-seph, for ev - er blessed. They tra-vel wea-ri-ly

An orchestral arrangement of this piece scored for harp, 2 percussion, and strings in F minor is available on rental from the Publisher.

Copyright © 2008, Oxford University Press, Inc. Photocopying this copyright material is ILLEGAL.

to my friend A. Talazac

5. Noël
Christmas

Victor Wilder (1835–92)
trans. Jane Marsh

GABRIEL FAURÉ
(1845–1924)

Liaison suggestions

M. 4, *Le givre aux* (sounds like girvr'_o); **m. 7**, *Et dans les airs* (sounds like lez air); **m. 8**, *le vol des anges éveille un bruit mystérieux* (sounds like voldez_angez éveiy_un); **mm. 16 & 17**, *chaumiere ou* (sounds like shomyer'_oo); **mm. 20 & 21**, *ses yeux* (sounds like sez yeux); **mm. 25 & 26**, *Sourit aux* (sounds like soorit_o); **mm. 36–38**, *Comme eux, o people inclinetoi* (sounds like Comm'_eux, ô peupl'_inclinetoi); **m. 39**, *pieux exemple* (sounds like pieux_exemple); **mm. 41–43**, *Car cette é table, cette un Temple, Et cet enfant* (sounds like Car cett' é table, cett'_un Temple, Et cet_enfant).

Copyright © 2008, Oxford University Press, Inc. Photocopying this copyright material is ILLEGAL.

7. Der Hirten Lied am Krippelein
The Shepherds' Song at the Little Crib

C. F. Daniel Schubart (1739–91)
trans. Jane Marsh

J. C. G. LOEWE (1796–1869)
arr. F. H. Schneider

to Julia Ivanovna Mussorgsky

8. Molitva
Prayer

Mikhail Lermontov (1814–41)
translit. and trans. Jane Marsh

MODEST MUSSORGSKY
(1839–81)

*Russian church music observes a's and o's to be sung as written, unlike conversational Russian. The use of an apostrophe indicates that the preceding consonant is to be pronounced softly, and when used with *Mater'* (m. 9), *vrutchit'* (m. 26–27), *molodost'* (m. 45), *starost'* (m. 47), it denotes a single, soft, and quick sound combination of t and y. *Ny-n'yeh* (m. 11) is pronounced nuhée-nyeh, *pustynnuyu* (m. 19–20) is pronounced pu-stuhée-nuyu, *polnych* (m. 43) is pronounced pol-nuhéehch. The hch, in *hchotchu* (m. 28–29) and *hcholodnogo* (m. 34–5), sounds like the German (or Russian) Ch, as in *Ach*, preceded by an h. *Shchastiyem* (m. 38) is pronounced shas-ti-yem and *shchastya* (m. 39) is pronounced shas-tya. Both word beginnings have the *a* sounding more like the *a* in 'at' than that in 'father'.

Copyright © 2008 Oxford University Press, Inc. Photocopying this copyright material is ILLEGAL.

9. Maria am Rosenstrauch
Mary at the Rose Shrub

E. L. Schellenberg (1883–1964)
trans. Jane Marsh

MAX REGER
(1873–1916)

10. Venitelo a vedere 'l mi' piccino
O come and look at him, my little baby

Arturo Birga
trans. Jane Marsh

OTTORINO RESPIGHI
(1879–1936)

*The text of this song is in a Tuscan vernacular. The following enunciation guide will assist the singer in proper pronunciation of the text.

Mm. 1 & 2; *Venitelo a vedere 'l mi' piccino* (il mio), enunciating both words –'l and mi'– in vernacular, as though complete words, flowing with composed rhythm
M. 18; *al dolce mi' tesoro* (mio), only enough notes composed for this vernacular abbreviation
M. 22; *ha mosso 'l labbro al* (il labbro), eliding... ha mosso 'l and doubling the l's ('l and labbro)..., create this vernacular abbreviation; then eliding labbro al to finish the sentence
M. 24 & 25; *vio su'n Paradiso* (in), only enough notes composed for this vernacular abbreviation

Copyright © 2008, Oxford University Press, Inc. Photocopying this copyright material is ILLEGAL.

11. Die Allmacht
The Almighty

Johann Ladislaus Pyrker (1772–1847)
trans. Jane Marsh

FRANZ SCHUBERT
(1797–1828)

Copyright © 2008, Oxford University Press, Inc. Photocopying this copyright material is ILLEGAL.

12. Weihnachtlied
Christmas Song

Hans Christian Anderson (1805–75)
trans. Jane Marsh

ROBERT SCHUMANN
(1810–56)

Als das Christkind ward zur Welt gebracht, das uns von der Hölle gerettet, da lag's auf der Krippe bei finsterer Nacht, auf Stroh und Heu gebettet; doch über der Hütte glänzte der Stern, und der Ochse küsste den Fuss des Herrn. Halleluja, Kind Jesus!

As the Jesus Child was born to light, he saved us from hell and destruction, he lay in his crib, by the darkest night, on straw and hay, his cushion; and over the houses glowed the star, and the oxen kissed the foot of the Lord. Alleluia, Child Jesus!

Copyright © 2008, Oxford University Press, Inc. Photocopying this copyright material is ILLEGAL.

13. Ave Maria
Hail Mary

Dante Alighieri (1265–1321)
trans. Jane Marsh

GIUSEPPE VERDI
(1813–1901)

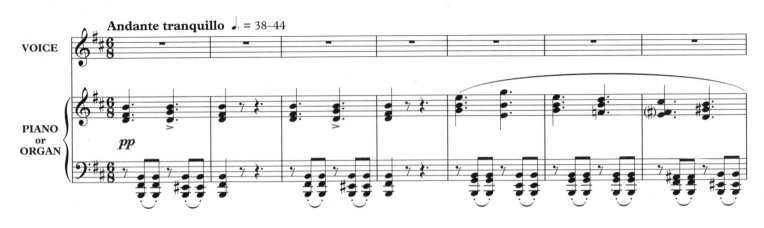

A - ve re - gi - na___ Ver - gi - ne Ma - ri - a,___ Pie - na di gra - zia: Id-
O hail our Sov - 'reign___ bless - ed Vir - gin Ma - ry,___ and full of mer - cy: God

Copyright © 2008 Oxford University Press, Inc. Photocopying this copyright material is ILLEGAL.

14. Schlafendes Jesuskind
Sleeping Jesus Child

Eduard Friedrich Mörike (1804–75)
trans. Jane Marsh

HUGO WOLF
(1860–1903)

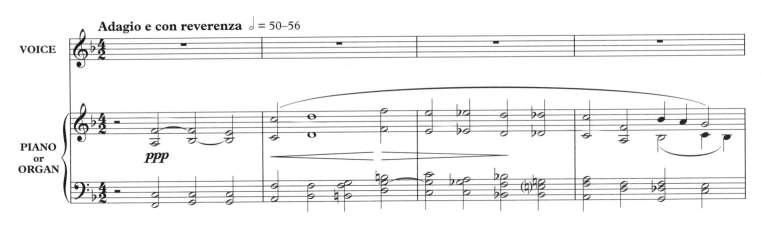

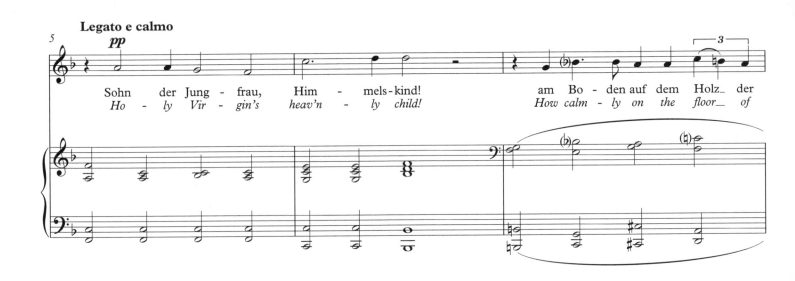

Sohn der Jungfrau, Himmels-kind! am Boden auf dem Holz der
Holy Virgin's heav'n-ly child! How calm-ly on the floor of

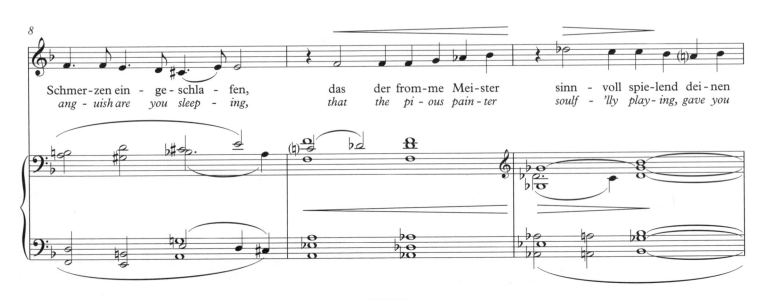

Schmerzen ein-ge-schla-fen, das der from-me Mei-ster sinn-voll spie-lend dei-nen
ang-uish are you sleep-ing, that the pi-ous pain-ter soulf-'lly play-ing, gave you

Copyright © 2008, Oxford University Press, Inc. Photocopying this copyright material is ILLEGAL.